Adventure
Travel Tips

Advice for the adventure of a lifetime

Suzanne Swedo

FALCON®

A FALCON GUIDE®

Falcon® Publishing is continually expanding its list of recreational guidebooks. All books include detailed descriptions, accurate maps, and all information necessary for enjoyable trips. You can order extra copies of this book and get information and prices for other Falcon® books by writing Falcon, P.O. Box 1718, Helena, MT 59624, or by calling toll-free 1-800-582-2665. Also, please ask for a copy of our current catalog. Visit our website at www.Falcon.com or contact us by e-mail at falcon@falcon.com.

Cover photo by Wolfgang Kaehler.

Library of Congress Cataloging-in-Publication Data

Swedo, Suzanne, 1945-
    Adventure travel tips : advice for the adventure of a lifetime / Suzanne Swedo.
        p. cm. -- (A Falcon guide)
    ISBN 1-56044-982-9
    1. Outdoor recreation. 2. Ecotourism. I. Title. II. Series.

GV191.6 .S89 2001
910--dc21
                                                                00-066296

CAUTION

Outdoor recreational activities are by their very nature potentially hazardous. All participants in such activities must assume responsibility for their own actions and safety. The information contained in this guidebook cannot replace sound judgment and good decision-making skills, which help reduce exposure, nor does the scope of this book allow for the disclosure of all the potential hazards and risks involved in such activities.

Learn as much as possible about the outdoor recreational activities in which you participate, prepare for the unexpected, and be cautious. The reward will be a safer and more enjoyable experience.

♻ Text pages printed on recycled paper.

For Melinda

Acknowledgments

Thanks to all those who contributed their advice, expertise, and research materials to help produce this book, especially Singaman Lama and Melinda Goodwater at Goodwaters Adventures; Kathleen Anderson at Wintermoon; Kate McClain at Blue Waters; Conrad Hirsh at Remote River Expeditions; and Pete Warner at the Adventurous Traveler Bookstore. Thanks also to the National Outings Committee of the Sierra Club, and to fellow travelers, supporters, and friends like Nan Kaeser, Laura Lathrop, Larry Guss, Sherry Rogers, Pat Medley, and, as always, Rex Raymer.

Contents

Introduction

WHAT IS ADVENTURE TRAVEL?

All travel is adventure in a sense. Whenever you leave home for the purpose of experiencing new sights and sounds, people and places, even if purely passively from the window of a tour bus, you are embarking on an adventure of a sort. Adventure travel as defined today, however, is what used to be the province of the intrepid, square-jawed type, clad in khaki and pith helmet, setting off to "conquer" or "tame" some section of the earth previously unknown to "civilized" western society.

There aren't too many places left unknown to anybody apart from their native inhabitants anymore, and a new ethic of respecting and celebrating the diversity of life on earth has replaced the former desire to convert or subdue everything and everybody within reach. Still, the need for physical, intellectual, and emotional challenge and stimulation persists. When you immerse yourself in a new and foreign environment where there is a degree of physical risk involved and when you have challenges to overcome, all your senses are engaged. You become attentive to every detail; your awareness of the world and of yourself is heightened and you experience each moment to the fullest. It is then that you feel most energized and fully alive.

Some are content with vicarious, passive adventure through television or the written word, or contrived risks and thrills in the form of bungee jumping, war games,

1

motorcycle racing, or even riding a roller-coaster. Others, perhaps like you, become adventure travelers. Unlike the traditional tourist who wishes to maintain, or even exceed, his usual level of comfort, you seek more complete and active immersion in a new environment and welcome new experiences that may lead to fundamental changes in yourself, your attitudes, beliefs, and priorities.

Adventure travel most often takes you away from cities, luxury hotels, and restaurants (often from *any* hotels and restaurants). It usually means relinquishing the safety net of social services you are used to like sanitation, professional medical care, and law enforcement.

Most adventure travel, especially that branch known as ecotourism, is consciously environmentally sensitive. Travelers attempt to leave the least possible evidence of their passing through the earth's wild places and to consume the smallest possible quantity of local resources. This usually means that accommodations are simpler and more primitive, that groups are smaller, and that locomotion is slower and less "efficient." Such travel frequently, though not always, involves more vigorous physical activity: climbing, hiking, skiing, paddling, cycling, or riding a mule, a camel, or an elephant.

If you are a true adrenaline junky, you can shoot the rapids of Chile's notorious Bio Bio River in a rubber raft, scuba dive among the sharks off the Gold Coast of Australia, or toil up a Himalayan glacier with rope and ice axe. If you relish danger with a human face, you can visit the world's political hotspots and hobnob with soldiers and revolutionaries on a "Reality Tour," or choose a destination from Fielding's *The World's Most Dangerous Places* (see Appendix B).

You may be a collector of experiences with a desire to climb the Seven Summits (the highest mountain peak on each of the continents). You may be a list-keeper like the devoted birder who spends huge sums and suffers great inconvenience to add a new species to her life list. You may seek adventure and personal enrichment through learning: digging for archeological treasures in the Middle East, banding birds in Panama, counting bighorn sheep in the American West. You may wish to do good and have fun at the same time by helping to build a school in Nepal, teaching English in Ecuador, nursing orphaned orangutans in Borneo. You can grunt with the gorillas in central Africa, explore the volcanoes of Iceland, the geysers of Yellowstone or New Zealand, or the cloud forests of Venezuela. You can ride a covered wagon across the West, participate in a real cattle roundup, sail the Turkish coast, hike the Inca Trail, paddle an outrigger in the South Pacific, follow the Silk Road across Asia. You can even enroll in astronaut training so you will be ready when space travel becomes available to the public.

If you can imagine it, there is likely an organization out there to help you do it or a book to tell you how.

1

Are You an Adventure Traveler?

The most important characteristic of an adventure traveler is a good attitude. You must be, first and foremost, flexible and adaptable. You must be energetic but patient, curious but discreet and sensitive, accepting and tolerant, but not gullible. You must be, above all, self-sufficient and responsible. And you must have a sense of humor.

In wilderness anyplace in the world you will be subject to nature's whims, particularly unexpected weather changes that can force a change in itinerary or timetable. Even in cities, international travel seldom goes smoothly. Sooner or later luggage will get lost or delayed, connections missed, reservations bungled. You must be able to take it all in stride; embrace the unpredictable. Recognize the fact that the "mañana" attitude shared by many people in the world's less industrialized regions is real. Other cultures do not share our preoccupation with speed, efficiency, and punctuality, but take life as it comes.

Most adventures involve waiting. It may be in a blind in a jungle for a tiger to show up, or on a makeshift landing strip on the tundra for your bush pilot to arrive, or for the bus to carry you to Outer Someplace-or-Other. How do you handle standing in line at the bank at home or sitting in traffic on the freeway? Are you prepared to suffer more of the same in an unfamiliar environment? Are you ready, on the other hand, to spring into action at a moment's notice when the tiger appears or the bus arrives?

You might have to adapt to different standards of cleanliness. You may have to subsist on unfamiliar, sometimes unrecognizable foods, served or eaten at different times and different intervals than you are used to. You may need to balance the desire to avoid giving offense by accepting some native dish of doubtful freshness or doneness against your own continued good health.

You must be willing to accept the fact that some of the values you thought were universal among human beings are in fact the products of your own culture. Even physical gestures that seem instinctive have different meanings to different people. It's up to you to do your best to find out in advance what constitutes proper behavior, and when you get to your destination to be alert to people's interactions among themselves and with you.

Wilderness environments as well as developing countries often lack the safety nets you expect at home. Medical facilities may be few or nonexistent. There might be no search-and-rescue apparatus in place if you get into trouble. Adventure travelers must have a good sense of when to trust and when to be wary of other people. What is your record at home? Are you open and friendly, willing to ask questions? Can you trust your own instincts when your suspicions are aroused? Your attitude at home will accompany you on your adventure. Can you retain your composure and your good judgment when you are tired or stressed?

In many parts of the world civil unrest of one kind or another is always possible, though it is seldom completely unexpected. It is rare for travelers to become embroiled in local conflicts, but it can and does happen. (Some people actually seek out such situations, whether for humanitarian reasons or simple thrill seeking.) Will apprehension about the possibility of such events spoil your vacation? If so, don't head for areas of potential trouble, and don't travel alone.

What adventure travelers are *not* are people who enjoy a strict schedule of pre-planned "activities" primarily consisting of gazing out of the window of an air-conditioned bus or trooping in docile herds to this or that "point of interest" to be given a canned lecture from a bored guide, escorted back to a hotel with food and furnishings indistinguishable from those back home, to socialize with folks also indistinguishable from the friends and neighbors they left behind.

Travelers off the beaten path will have to do more preparation and take on more personal responsibility than those on a conventional tour, but are sure to find the rewards to be exponentially greater. The more effort you expend in your search for adventure, the more joy you'll find, guaranteed!

My adventure

At the beginning of a journey down the Omo River in Ethiopia, each participant was handed two essential pieces of equipment: a croc-knocker, and a tsetse fly swatter. The fly swatter needs no explanation. The river was full of crocodiles, and we were instructed to bash at the water if one approached the raft too closely. When a croc did launch an attack, there was no time to take up cudgels; it happened in an instant. We had just touched the shore and were about to pull up onto the riverbank to camp for the night. There was a splash and a chomp, and a huge section of the raft began to hiss and deflate. I do not remember jumping from the raft, but somehow we all reached the beach and nobody was hurt. We later discovered that we had pulled up onto the shore at a point between the mother croc in the water and her nest full of eggs buried in the mud. She was only warning us away from her young and did not repeat her attack. Still, we were so nervous that night that we took turns at croc-watch. I remember huddling by a tiny fire at 2 AM, swatting flies in the damp heat and casting anxious glances toward the riverbank where several pairs of reptilian eyes reflected the firelight. I thought of what a great tale this would be to tell the folks back home if I survived the experience.

My adventure

In the 1970s my husband and I landed in a small town in the highlands of New Guinea on our way to Madang, a larger town near the mouth of the Sepik River. From there we would continue by boat to Kar Kar Island, about twenty-five miles off the coast, to work on a cocoa plantation. Near the airstrip was a sort of general store—tiny, but comprehensive. On display were items as varied as beer, bandages, shovels, cooking pots, sugar, tea, toothpaste, cameras, radios, tape recorders, and towels. There in a crowded aisle, we squeezed by a local shopper who was comparing prices and features of electronic calculators. He wore a beautiful feathered headdress, some sort of bone in his nose, a necklace of pig tusks, and nothing else at all. We paid for our sodas, he paid for his calculator and some tobacco. He carried his pipe tucked through a hole in his earlobe since he had no pockets. We never did figure out where he kept his cash.

2

Some Practical Considerations of Time and Money

Do not choose something that looks like adventure travel or ecotourism because you think camping must be cheaper than staying in a hotel. There are some very posh tent safaris with servants galore in some very remote places. Adventure travel is often more expensive because of complicated logistics: getting to places not served by mass transportation, paying guides or others with special skills, or obtaining expensive permits. Some countries with subsistence economies, such as Nepal, rely on tourism to bring in cash and charge hefty sums to climb their famous peaks or visit formerly forbidden regions. Since this kind of travel is unpredictable (if it were predictable, it wouldn't be an adventure, would it?) there are more likely to be unexpected expenses such as accommodations or food on unscheduled layovers. In addition, there may be considerable outlay in specialized clothing or equipment, whether you buy it yourself, rent it, or pay for its use indirectly by paying higher prices charged by the outfitter to cover their purchase and maintenance of gear.

Adventure travel usually requires more time than conventional tourism as well. Transportation to remote regions is more complicated and usually slower; and transportation within developing countries is frequently unreliable, even if the air carrier, for example, is based in and managed from a super-efficient European country. Your vehicle, whether a bus, dugout canoe, camel, or balloon may be late, may arrive and leave before schedule, or may not show up at all. There is always a chance of missing connections. In the wilderness of your own country, bad weather, high water, difficult route-finding, accident, or illness can slow you down. Extra time should be built into any itinerary.

3

On Your Own or with an Outfitter?

There are some places you simply can't get to on your own—at least legally. Sure, there are tales of travelers who have disguised themselves as natives, as men or women, as monks or soldiers, who have managed to slip across some forbidden border to mingle undetected with the locals for years. Such adventures, however, take more time and know-how (including knowledge of the language) than most of us have at our disposal. If you think you are ready for such an expedition, you probably don't need this book. (For great vicarious adventures along these lines, try Alexandra David Neel's *Magic and Mystery in Tibet* or Richard Burton's *Personal Narrative of a Pilgrimage to Almandinah and Mecca*.)

Some countries, like China/Tibet, Bhutan, and Burma, prohibit unescorted access to private individuals for political reasons. Environmentally sensitive destinations like the Galapagos Islands prohibit independent travel to protect fragile ecosystems. Some governments or government agencies require that visitors engage a local guide in order to bring a little money into the local economy. Then there are special cases like Antarctica which, under the Antarctic Treaty, is designated an international laboratory for scientific research, where no nation may stake a territorial claim.

11

Tourists stay on military bases (which exist only to provide logistic support for scientific research), or eat and sleep on cruise ships and visit the continent only on day-trips. There is no apparatus to deal with customs or immigration, no real hotels, stores, or restaurants.

Solo or informal group travel in some of the earth's uninhabited or extremely inhospitable regions is impractical, if not impossible, due to complicated logistics. In some high mountains, deserts, or on open ocean, a traveler must be completely self-contained. Everything needed for life— food, water, shelter, fuel, and some means for carrying it all—is often more than one or even several individuals can manage.

Some destinations are open to individual travelers in principle, but are so rigidly controlled by rules and regulations that a commercial outfitter is the only reasonable choice. Rafting the Colorado River through the Grand Canyon is a magical, exciting, and much too popular wilderness adventure. The National Park Service enforces a strict quota on the number of parties it allows on the river at one time. This insures that every visitor gets a true wilderness experience and the river environment does not become degraded through overuse. The wait list for private parties who wish to run the river is currently ten years long and involves a hefty fee. If you don't want to wait that long, sign up with a commercial outfitter who already has a permit. It will cost more, of course, but part of the price covers the permit fee the outfitter also pays.

Aside from exceptions like these, plenty of the world's wild places welcome, or at least admit, all kinds of travelers, from those on organized commercial expeditions to foot-loose free spirits. Which way do you like to travel?

TIME AND MONEY

The obvious financial advantage of traveling on your own is, of course, that you will not have to pay an outfitter, who must in turn, pay its guides, its office overhead and, if it is a commercial company, make a profit. It is possible to travel on next to nothing if you have plenty of time and realistic expectations. You should be an extremely healthy and hardy soul with a cast-iron digestive system, who can travel on stand-by or in the off-season and hitch rides when needed. You should be comfortable curling up for the night in a train station or behind a barn, subsisting on local food and surviving local standards of sanitation, or lack thereof.

However, if economy is your primary consideration in choosing to travel on your own, and if you do not fit the above description, do your research and calculations very carefully. There's a good chance that traveling with a group, even a commercial one, will save you money.

In the first place, you'll benefit from group rates on air-fare and accommodations. Second, your major expenses will have been paid for in advance, so you won't have any unpleasant surprises once your journey is underway. An outfitter's experience, know-how, and local contacts can mean considerable savings, too. They probably have already scouted out the best values in accommodations, food, and transport. They will be able to help with local currency in other countries and will know what the going rates for services and souvenirs should be. On your own, you'll be at the mercy of the rickshaw/taxi/bus driver or shopkeeper who insists his cousin or brother-in-law can get you a special deal (frequently at twice the usual price) on this or that. The outfitter also knows whom to pay baksheesh, whom to tip, and how much.

If your journey requires the use of special equipment such as a kayak or a life preserver, it will probably be included in the cost of a commercial outing. Tents and sleeping bags may be included, too. Completely equipping yourself on your own, especially with gear you will seldom use again, if at all, can be prohibitively expensive.

An outfitter can also help you save by providing a list of what you will really need to bring, and what you will not. You won't be compelled to buy something indispensable at last-minute inflated prices when you get there, and you will be less likely to be seduced by unnecessary and expensive gadgets shown in slick travel catalogs or stores.

Sometimes you can sign up for a tour that includes transportation and even accommodations, then make use of just what you need, and go your own way the rest of the time. You could still come out ahead financially. If you have the time and money, go with a group the first time, get the lay of the land, learn the ropes, and come back again on your own and do it *your* way. For most travelers, time is as valuable a commodity as cash.

You may decide that you can travel more efficiently and have more time to do exactly as you like on your own. You may not be willing to spend time on some activity or in some location that doesn't interest you, but is part of a set itinerary. As a rule, everything takes longer in a group. There is always somebody who overslept, has to go to the bathroom at the last minute, or forgot something and must go back to the last rest stop to retrieve it. You can usually start earlier, cover more ground, and see and do more by yourself. On the other hand, when you travel with a professional guide service, you can avoid frustrating hours figuring out how to get someplace or do something, getting lost, or becoming entangled in red tape in the form of permits or travel documents. Accommodations and meals will be arranged in advance on an escorted trip and you don't have to seek out a place to sleep or eat each day. Transportation will already be arranged, at least from the official starting point of the journey. (In most cases, transportation from your home to wherever your group meets will not be included in the trip cost. A good outfitter will furnish suggestions about the best way to get there, and they may have connections with travel agents or airlines with which they have worked before who can help to smooth your way and may offer a discount to boot.)

Much of what you are paying the commercial company for is advance planning. If you are among those who enjoy the planning process as much as the actual journey and have the time and patience to do the necessary homework, you might have more fun preparing and traveling on your own.

It's a big job, though. You will need to learn at least a few essential words and phrases in the local language if it isn't your own, understand the currency and exchange rates, and learn enough about the land to plan a viable itinerary and to pack properly. You will need to understand enough about the laws and traditions of the culture, if different from your own, to avoid giving insult or offense, and to learn basic survival skills, such as how to find food and shelter and how to doctor yourself if necessary. There are lots of books and publications out there to help. Check out Falcon Publishing and the Adventurous Traveler Bookstore for a good selection. (See Appendix B.)

An experienced outfitter will let you know what to bring, what kind of paperwork in the way of visas or permits or immunizations you will need and how to get them, along with anything else that is especially important for you to know. All you have to do is follow instructions, call the cat/dog/houseplant sitter, and pack.

PERSONALITY AND TEMPERAMENT

Every bit as important as time and money are matters of personality and temperament. If you don't have a good time on your vacation, saving time and money is irrelevant. Some people are suited to travel in groups, others are happier alone.

Know thyself! Some people (probably a minority) are just natural loners who are comfortable in their own company and prefer to savor their new experiences in solitude. Others find experiences richer and more rewarding when shared. Close your eyes and picture yourself on your perfect vacation. Do you see yourself solitary and content beside your flickering lantern in the evening recording your thoughts in your journal? Or do you see yourself as part of a cozy group reliving the shared events of the day around the campfire?

When you travel on your own you have greater flexibility to change your mind and your plans, to linger in a place you enjoy, and to move on when you have had enough. You do not have to follow somebody else's agenda. On the other hand, you may prefer a vacation that has enough structure to leave you free from the need to make decisions or take responsibility, to relax and go with the flow. Questions of independence and flexibility should be weighed against the sense of security and safety that group travel affords. There will be help in an emergency if you are ill or injured, and somebody to ask for advice in difficult situations.

Signing up for a group outing is a great way to meet and make new friends. People who are, like yourself, committed to climb a mountain or run a river are more likely to be adventurous and interesting companions whose company will enhance your own enjoyment. Still, the (usually remote) possibility exists that you will end up with an obnoxious roommate or tentmate. How much will that affect your enjoyment of the whole experience?

How important to your sense of well-being is privacy? Many westerners are not prepared for the fact that privacy is not a concept understood in many Third World countries where overpopulation is extreme and the family or village is all-important. In truly remote regions, you will probably find yourself the center of attention wherever you go, surrounded by throngs of curious children (and sometimes adults) who follow you behind bushes or peek through gaps in your tent when you want to be alone. Individual travelers may be less conspicuous than a group, and may not draw so much attention, but on the other hand, your group, leaders, and staff may provide a buffer between you and your public when you really need it.

Of course, one of the joys of travel of any kind is meeting the natives. Some feel that travel with a group isolates them and prevents as much contact with local people as they would like. However, you might also find that you get to know the locals better with a group than on your own. Your trip leader should already have contacts with people who live in the area and know how to arrange introductions and visits. Furthermore, a good company will use local people as at least part of its staff, people you will be dealing with every day. You'll get to learn about their families and lives in greater depth and may develop international friendships that last for years.

Wildlife watchers may believe that as individuals they can move more quietly than a group can, and are more likely to see the leopard in the bush or the lyrebird on its branch alone. Still, if this is the object of your journey, your guide probably knows where the leopard roams or the lyrebird perches in the first place, and may increase your odds of seeing it. You will probably learn more about the environment with a guide and others who are knowledgeable themselves, especially if you join a university or museum-sponsored outing whose primary purpose is educational.

My adventure

Flying into Dar es Salaam, a notoriously dangerous city (ironically, its name means "Haven of Peace") my seatmate informed me that there was some sort of meeting or convention in town, and that there were no hotel rooms available. I had previously been assured that Dar es Salaam always had lots of empty rooms, and so I made no hotel reservations. The airport was some distance from town, had no facilities, and would be a dangerous place to sleep. When I told him about my predicament, he went into action. He was being picked up by his company's limo and driven to town. He took me along and called friends, a young couple with two children who lived in the suburbs. I had a comfy bed for the night and a good dinner in exchange for a painless evening of babysitting while the couple enjoyed a long-overdue evening out alone.

4

Choosing an Outfitter

If you have decided to join an organized expedition, and have determined where and when to go and how much time and money you can spend, you're ready to pick an outfitter. Thousands of adventure travel companies have sprung up in the last couple of decades, so you will need to allow yourself plenty of time to survey the field and make the best choice. Do not make the mistake of signing up for an outing merely because it fits your schedule and goes to the right country. If you are like most people, this isn't something you do often; perhaps it's truly a once-in-a-lifetime experience. Make it count.

Before you start poring over catalogs, consider the time of year you plan to travel and remember that the part of the world you want to visit may have a completely different weather pattern than the part you where you live. In the Southern Hemisphere, the seasons are reversed. Summer is the traditional travel season for most of us in North America, especially teachers and families with children, but it is not the season to explore Patagonia (unless you especially crave darkness, snow, and ice). In some parts of the world, summer is also monsoon season where it rains every day. Off-season travel may be a good way to save money, but if the scenery is going to be obscured by clouds from the first day to the last, you might as well stay home.

Be realistic about what you can accomplish in the time you have to spend. Compare the times allowed by different outfitters for the same trip. If they cover the same territory in very different spans of time, find out why. On a typical Himalayan trek, for example, it takes two days of flying (including an unavoidable stopover) to reach Kathmandu, then you need another day for final preparations and obtaining the proper documents, then most likely at least one day more by land or air to reach your trailhead. Add a few more days at the end of your trek to do everything in reverse, and you find that in order to do a three-week trek, you actually have to allow four full weeks.

Make sure that the amount of money in your travel budget will cover, in addition to the land cost shown in the outfitter's catalog, your transportation to the meeting place, and plenty more for unanticipated expenses. Plan generously for those unexpected extras, then factor in a little more besides. And don't forget that there are still parts of the world where you cannot use a credit card.

Now all you have to do is decide where you want to go, what you want to do there, and with whom you want to go. There are so many options that you're sure to find one that suits you perfectly, but it may take some research. If your goal is some part of the world so remote and obscure that only a very few companies go there at all, the field will be narrowed considerably. Except for the giants like Mountain Travel/Sobek who go just about everywhere, outfitters and guides usually specialize in one particular part of the world, the one they know best.

Winnowing out the companies that don't go to your chosen destination is the first step. Then you can narrow down the field still further by considering the following questions: What do you want to do when you get there? Are you a hiker, a climber, a paddler, a cyclist, a skier, or strictly a sightseer? Do you plan to do lots of photography, sketching, writing, studying, teaching, helping people in need? What are your interests? Wild animals, birds, people, history, flowers, art, literature, mythology, geology? There are organizations specializing in all of these and even more you never dreamed of. You'll be happier and safer with a guide who understands and enjoys the same thing, and will have more fun among traveling companions whose interests and abilities are compatible with yours. Hikers or climbers eager to reach a distant peak will resent (or leave behind) the photographer who wants to stop and wait until the light on the lake is just right. If photography is your passion, pick a photo safari where everybody has the same expectations and priorities. Many of these are led by, or are in the company of, well-known professional photographers.

Are you a serious birder willing to spend long periods at a stretch in a muggy tropical forest scanning the treetops, uttering chirps and whistles in hopes of catching even a momentary glimpse of a new species? Or does the idea of such an activity sound unbearably tedious? Birders should investigate the National Audubon Society, The Nature Conservancy, a museum of natural history, or a university extension program. They conduct their own expeditions, and carry ads in their publications for other companies whose trips should appeal to the same kinds of people. Those with more general interests should check out catalogs for more general kinds of trips.

How active, energetic, and physically fit are you? Are you willing and able to hike for many miles through rough country to find the bird, or the rare orchid, or the ruins of the lost city? What is the maximum amount of inconvenience or downright physical discomfort you will be willing to undergo to get there? Will anxiety about sleeping on the ground, encountering creepy-crawlies, and handling the lack of bathroom facilities dilute or destroy the pleasurable anticipation of reaching your goal? If the considerations make you uncomfortable then stick with outfitters whose literature emphasizes the luxury, comfort, and cleanliness of their accommodations. (Luxurious adventure travel is not necessarily an oxymoron.) If, on the other hand, overcoming challenges and testing your physical limits are what turn you on, try Outward Bound, NOLS (National Outdoor Leadership School), or some of the many schools of mountaineering.

Do you wish to travel with people whose backgrounds, values, lifestyles, or special needs are sure to be compatible with your own? There are a wide variety of companies and organizations that specialize in adventure travel for, among others, vegetarians, women, seniors, gays, singles, families, nudists, Christians, Jews, chocolate lovers, or people with disabilities. See Appendix B for some examples.

SOURCES OF INFORMATION

While your usual travel agent may be quite helpful in planning and booking conventional kinds of trips for you, few are very knowledgeable about active travel off the beaten path. You'll probably have to do most of the research yourself. The richest source of information by far is, of course, the Internet. You can click on adventure travel and eco-tourism in general and you can click on a specific country, activity, interest, or outfitter. You can read the day-by-day journals and see photos by travelers who have been there and done just what you want to do, find out what they liked or didn't like, what they took along, what they used and what they didn't. You can study an outfitter's website, then ask specific questions by e-mail not only of the outfitter, but of people who have traveled with that company.

If you do not have Internet access (or even if you do), check out periodicals like *Backpacker, Outside,* and *Escape.* They have lots of articles and advice about wilderness travel and carry ads for hundreds of outfitters. Special interest and nonprofit outdoor organizations who run their own outings, such as the Sierra Club, Audubon Society, Appalachian Mountain Club, and The Nature Conservancy, are the best bets for nature lovers seeking both local and international adventures.

The Specialty Travel Index (see Appendix B) provides contacts for adventure and special interest travel. It is used by travel agents to help find outfitters for their more active clients, but you can also subscribe yourself. It lists expeditions by destination, by activity, and by outfitter and is updated and distributed twice a year. It's also available on-line.

Of course, word-of-mouth recommendations are best of all, so long as you are well enough acquainted with your informant to know whether you enjoy the same things. Make sure your tastes, expectations, abilities, and interests are similar. Ask specific questions about what they did, what they liked about it, and why.

Once you have gathered enough material, narrow the field down to a manageable number of options, perhaps a half-dozen or so of the most intriguing trips. Then read all the literature very carefully. A good, long-established company's brochure should spell out everything in very concrete terms. If they have been in business a long time, they will understand exactly what you will want to know and will have it covered in detail in their literature, or will have it at their fingertips when you call. If the office staff doesn't know the answers to your questions, they should be able to refer you to somebody who does. If possible, talk with the person who will be your guide. (Remember that the guide may be out in the field doing his or her job of guiding, and may be hard to reach. That's another good reason to begin your trip-planning early.)

COMPARING ADVENTURE TRAVEL COMPANIES

Here is a list of questions to consider when selecting the perfect outfitter for your adventure:

How long has the company been in business? Choose a reliable, experienced, well-established outfitter.

Has the company done this specific trip before? Have they had time to make the necessary local contacts and learn the customs of the country?

How large are their groups? More than fifteen people can be unwieldy, even if there are enough guides to watch out for everybody. Bigger groups are noisier and more obtrusive and may be harder on the environment, especially if wildlife watching or mixing with locals is an important objective.

Are there an adequate number of staff people to keep everything running smoothly and to handle emergencies if they should arise?

Is at least one of the guides a local person who speaks the language, is known and trusted by local people and understands the land?

Who are these guides? How long have they been with the company? How many times have they done this particular trip? You don't want to be stuck with somebody who is the world's foremost expert on orangutans or kangaroos but lacks the social skills and the good judgment to keep a group of travelers safe and happy. On the other hand, a charming, charismatic leader who knows nothing about the environment or its people or is generally incompetent is equally undesirable.

What is the company's safety record? Have they had many injuries or illnesses? How have they handled them? Could they have been avoided? Is the staff trained in first aid? What kind of safety and sanitary measures do they ordinarily take? How much liability insurance do they carry?

Is the company environmentally and culturally responsible? Do they use local help and try to support the local economy? Are they careful about litter, pollution, and conservation of natural resources? In a poor country suffering from deforestation where people live at a subsistence level, is the group completely self-sufficient for fuel and food so they will not contribute to local problems? Are guides committed to a policy of keeping an adequate distance from wildlife to avoid disrupting their normal behavior?

What else will the outfitter do for you? Do they arrange for visas and other travel documents? Do they furnish instructions and guidelines to help you do it yourself? Do they provide a detailed list of suggested clothing and equipment? Do they provide maps and general information about your destination? How about a bibliography of supplemental reading material? Will they help arrange your flights or other transportation from home so that if there are delays or cancellations, you will still be able to connect with your trip?

Ask the company for a few references from people who have traveled with them in the past. Of course, you will only be referred to satisfied customers, but you can ask more specific questions of them than whether or not they had a good time. You may get a better feel for the general flavor or style of the trip. Some companies treat clients as pampered guests even in the Amazonian jungle or the African savanna. Others welcome, or even encourage, more active participation on the part of trip members. Ask former clients what a typical day was like, and where and when did they go. Also ask who the guides were; how the weather was; what the food was like; and is there anything you should know that wasn't covered in the information received from the outfitter.

GETTING SPECIFIC

Make sure you understand the outfitter's terminology, and be sure to study the fine print.

How much time will you actually spend on this adventure doing whatever it is you signed up to do? On a kayaking journey or an elephant safari, will you be spending most of your time paddling or riding? Or will there be several days of more conventional forms of travel with an hour (or several) now and then on the river or in the howdah (saddle)? In the Arctic, will you be deposited on the dogsled and driven from place to place, or do you help feed, harness, and drive the dogs?

What exactly is included in the trip cost? As mentioned above, transportation from your home to the actual starting point is usually, though not always, your responsibility. Is all transport from that point on part of the trip cost? What about accommodations and meals between flights? Airport taxes? Fees for permits? Insurance? (See page XX.) On "free" days, do you have to pay for your own meals? What about optional activities? Who pays for those? Does the outfitter furnish any special equipment you might need as part of the published cost, or do they have some available for rent, or do you have to bring your own? What, exactly, is their cancellation policy? Most companies charge a cancellation fee to cover their own administrative costs. When is the latest you can cancel and receive a full refund, aside from the cancellation fee? Can you cancel later than that and get part of your money back? Even more important, what happens if the outfitter cancels? Do they guarantee that the trip will take place no matter how many sign up? What is the minimum number? What is the last possible date they promise to inform you if the trip is cancelled so you'll have time to make other plans? Of course, if they cancel, you are entitled to every penny of your money back, unless there are exceptions somewhere in the fine print.

How should the difficulty ratings be interpreted? Easy, moderate, and strenuous mean very different things to an athlete and a couch potato. For instance, how many miles/hours per day will you be hiking and at what elevation? Is the going steep or level, smooth or rocky? If you are not sure whether a particular outing is within your abilities, let the outfitter know what your regular conditioning program is at home, and what kinds of travel you have done recently. Then ask how the expedition in question compares. Will it be more strenuous or less? Beware of an outfitter who does not seem interested in your physical fitness at all if the outing involves much physical activity. If they accept anybody who applies, they may be desperate for business, and not a good prospect.

5

Cultural Concerns

One of the greatest rewards of any kind of travel is reaching across language and cultural barriers to find common ground upon which to meet, mingle, and make new friends. Those who make no effort to understand or tolerate traditions different from their own deprive themselves of much of the richness of travel. Worse, they can leave behind feelings of resentment among the local people that poisons their attitudes toward travelers who come later. There is still no better advice for wanderers than the old cliché, "When in Rome, do as the Romans do" (at least to the best of your ability and understanding). Your purpose in visiting may be incomprehensible to the local people. Climbing a mountain may seem to them, at best, a ridiculous waste of energy, at worst, an offense to the gods who live on top. As a guest in their country and, if you are lucky, even in their homes, it is your responsibility to be extra alert and sensitive to whatever it is the Romans are doing and thinking. If you do not approve of the way things are done, do your best to go with the flow. You're entitled to your opinions but a vacation is not the time or place to make sweeping political or social changes.

If you are traveling with a group, your leader or local guide should fill you in on what is expected or what might give offense. If you are traveling on your own, do your

homework. Read something about the culture and traditions of the place before you go, and pay special attention to
what the locals do when you arrive. Do people take off their
shoes before entering a building? Do they take off their hats?
Put on their hats? Do they carefully avoid physical contact
with others, or hug and jostle one another freely? Some
practices are subtle and easy to miss. In much of the world,
only the right hand is used for eating or handling food; the
left is for other bodily functions and is considered unclean.
In many regions, blowing one's nose into the street is proper form; the western habit of snorting into a tissue and then
putting the whole mess back into one's pocket is thought
unspeakably disgusting.

Note that some of the things you assumed to be cultural universals may in fact vary from place to place. Gestures
that seem to be purely instinctive may have completely different meanings in different parts of the world. Beckoning
with one finger is a highly insulting gesture in some cultures, as is pointing with a finger. In India and parts of
Nepal, the side-to-side chin wag means "yes," not "no." In
other parts of Asia giggling often indicates embarrassment,
not ridicule.

Some of the things that are common to many cultures
may be expressed in a manner that you as an outsider do not
recognize. Americans, in particular, say "please" and "thank
you" at the drop of a hat, and may condemn people in other
countries as impolite because they do not use these words.
In fact, some languages have both a familiar form and a
polite form of making a request or expressing gratitude that

is built into the form of the language and do not need to tack on separate words.

A smile and an attempt to learn or use a word or two of the language, no matter how clumsily, helps to break the ice. Avoid passing out gifts or money, even if your intentions are the purest. Americans, in particular, are sometimes too generous, perhaps from guilt, perhaps from simple compassion for the very poor. Make sure you understand the consequences. You may be laying an impossible obligation on somebody who cannot afford to reciprocate, or you may be thought patronizing or condescending.

In some societies, begging is a legitimate activity, indeed, an opportunity for the giver to gain merit. It's okay for you to contribute as well, but don't give too much more than the locals do. Handing out toys and candy to children sometimes leads to begging of a different sort, which can escalate to demanding gifts from future travelers, who are met with anger when they refuse and causes them to form a bad impression of the country. Instead, share photos of your home and family. If you have skills or talents like sketching, playing a musical instrument, or juggling, share those, too.

Always ask whether somebody minds having his or her picture taken. Usually pointing at your camera and asking "Okay?" is enough. In some very remote places people are still fearful of being photographed. In others, they will be happy to pose . . . for a fee. Sometimes people will ask to be photographed, and expect a copy of the results immediately, and do not understand that some cameras do not print out pictures on the spot. Do not promise to send photographs to anyone after you get home unless you can and will do so, and remember that if you promise one person in the village, you might have to promise everybody.

As always, at home or abroad, sensitivity and good will are important assets. It is usually safe to assume that others' intentions are benign unless you have good reason to believe otherwise. If somebody suddenly turns hostile for no apparent reason, consider that you might have made some social gaffe. Do not immediately respond with hostility on your own part that could escalate into a confrontation nobody wants.

My adventure

I joined an exploratory raft trip with Sobek (before the company joined forces with Mountain Travel) on a section of the Omo River in Ethiopia that had not previously been traveled. In some of the villages, the local people had seldom, if ever, seen anything like a rubber raft or pale skinned, pale-haired people who wore clothing. The women wore huge flat plates in their lower lips, and little else. We put on our friendliest smiles, but everyone seemed shy and a bit fearful, though extremely curious. A couple of the braver souls came forward and with one finger, tentatively touched the rafts, our clothing, hair, skin, but drew back again. One of our group suggested that we take off our clothes to demonstrate that we were also human, albeit oddly colored ones. It worked like a charm! We spent several days of delightful games, laughter, and learning about each other without benefit of a common language.

6

Adventure Travel Ethics

There is some dispute about the morality of adventure travel in general, especially that branch known as ecotourism. Some environmentalists fear that travel in sensitive environments will damage delicate habitats, disturb endangered wildlife, and disrupt indigenous people's way of life. Others believe that such travel is beneficial because it may encourage poor countries to preserve their wild places in order to attract tourist dollars instead of permanently destroying habitat by logging, mining, or overgrazing. Furthermore, those who have visited such unspoiled country, learned about its wildlife, and met its inhabitants may be motivated to add their voices to the protest against the ongoing destruction of the planet.

Responsible adventure travelers who plan to sign up with an outfitter should investigate the company's environmental policy and practices. Ask direct and specific questions about how the company contributes to the preservation of the environments they visit and sustains or improves the well-being of the local inhabitants. The fact that a company labels its outings "ecotours" or "nature tours" may be no more than a marketing ploy. You can investigate further by contacting any of several environmental watchdog organizations, some of which publish guidelines for choosing a responsible out-fitter, and keep files of reports on how previous clients have rated their performance. A few are listed in Appendix B.

Once your journey is underway, insist that local guides employed by the company comply with the stated guide-lines. Discourage guides who disturb the behavior of ani-mals or otherwise break the rules in order to give their clients a closer look in hopes of a earning a bigger tip.

Whether you travel with a group or on your own, you should be self-sufficient. Often the local people can barely feed themselves and do not have surplus food or fuel to sell. If you can help to support the economy by stocking up on local goods when they are abundant, so much the better, but do not become a burden on poor, though usually generous and hospitable, people.

Deforestation is a serious problem all over the world. It is especially important to supply your own cooking fuel in order to avoid cutting trees. In some regions, you must demonstrate to a government official that you have an ade-quate supply of your own before you may enter.

Only a few years ago, litter was unknown in poor areas. Every scrap of paper was salvaged and reused. Now plastic bags are found just about everyplace, but some countries have not yet developed an anti-litter ethic. Set a good exam-ple by not contributing to the mess and helping to clean up where you can.

Practice zero-impact camping methods wherever you go, whether or not the locals do. Camp, cook, and dispose of waste at the very least one hundred feet from water whenever possible. Pack out everything you packed in. Do not remove protected objects such as native artifacts and do not buy endangered plant and animal products. Refuse to patronize anybody who offers them for sale.

FINANCIAL MATTERS

Find out what the going rate is for some particular item or service you want or require, then determine whether or not bargaining is expected. While stinginess is never a virtue, paying too much for something can have negative consequences. Overpaying, especially because the seller seems to be so poor, can stir up bad feelings among friends and associates, and can lead to inflation. Prices rise, and travelers who come after you feel they are being overcharged and become resentful, and local people are unable to afford to buy necessities at foreign prices. Eventually, the relationship between host and guest can become no more than an opportunity for exploitation on both sides.

The same applies to tipping. Ask somebody in a position to know whether it is expected, and how much is appropriate. If it is not accepted practice, do not force money on someone who will be made uncomfortable, or even be insulted, by taking it.

BEING A CONSIDERATE TRAVELING COMPANION

In the wilderness or in an unfamiliar foreign environment, travelers often find themselves forced into closer and more constant contact with one another than they are used to. At the same time, they are more dependent upon each other for their well-being and sometimes even safety.

Tolerance and flexibility in dealing with your traveling companions is essential if everyone is to enjoy a smooth and successful expedition. Good preparation is also very important. Read and heed carefully all the material sent by the outfitter if you will be using one. Make sure your equipment is adequate so that somebody else won't have to share theirs, and keep your gear within prescribed weight and size limits so that somebody else doesn't have to take on part of your load as well as their own. Pay attention to meeting, waking, and eating times, so that others do not have to wait for you. If your trip involves strenuous activity, you owe it to yourself as well as to your traveling companions to be in good physical condition. Never sign up for an outing beyond your physical capability in order to "get in shape." You may prevent the rest of the group from keeping to its schedule and reaching the places and seeing the sights they have paid to see. You won't have a good time yourself if you become the problem trip member who is resented by everybody else.

If you will be traveling with a friend, a lover, or a family member, remember that the stress of adapting to a new environment can test even the closest of relationships. If you haven't traveled together before under these circumstances, perhaps a trial run on a weekend trip is in order. Discuss every possible contingency you can think of in advance so you can come to some agreement as to how you will deal with issues like finances, handling emergencies, goals and priorities, and even food preferences and sleeping habits.

7

Safety

Adventure travel in itself is probably slightly riskier than conventional tourism, but there aren't any reliable statistics available, partly because "adventure travel" isn't precisely defined. The list of activities that travel insurance policies will not cover might give you a clue about what is perceived to be dangerous by an organization willing to put its money on the line. These activities in themselves, however, aren't necessarily connected with travel. They would be dangerous—or not—wherever indulged in.

The issues that concern most prospective travelers are terrorism and civil unrest. The odds of becoming a victim of either are very slim, but not impossible. The fact that terrorist attacks appear in the news indicates that they do occur but are not common. A civil disturbance in a capital city or along a disputed border does not necessarily preclude travel anywhere in the country in question. Keep track of news reports about the place before you leave, and make use of the U.S. State Department's easily obtainable travel safety precautions. You can get these safety precautions by mail, telephone, or on-line through the Overseas Citizens Services. (See Appendix B.)

This information comes in three forms:

1. Travel Warnings: Issued when the State Department decides that Americans should avoid travel to a particular country.
2. Public Announcements: Warnings about specific, short-term dangers that could affect travelers anywhere such as bomb threats or anniversaries of certain terrorist events.
3. Consular Information Sheets: There is one for every country with information about any specific currency or immigration regulations, health hazards, possible disturbances, or recent criminal activity, along with locations of the embassy or consulate.

Another hazard, which you can neither predict nor control, is a natural disaster. Floods and earthquakes can occur anywhere, even at home. The best you can do, especially in a poor country with few emergency services, is to be as self-contained as possible. Make sure you always have some means of water purification and first aid skills and supplies. Get to an embassy or consulate if you can.

Ordinary garden-variety crime is more common than international terrorism, but at least there is more you can do to protect yourself. Read the Consular Information Sheets for the countries in which you plan to travel, but keep in mind that just because some particular form of criminal activity is mentioned there, you are not doomed to become a victim. Crime is universal, unfortunately, and Americans in particular should be aware that the United

States figures prominently in Fielding's *The World's Most Dangerous Places.*

These simple precautions, along with an application of ordinary common sense, can help to forestall any unpleasant experiences:

- read State Department warnings;
- tell somebody at home where you are going and when you are due back;
- make extra copies of passports and other important documents and stow them in different places;
- do not keep all your cash in the same place;
- leave unnecessary valuables such as jewelry at home, and keep large amounts of money and expensive items like cameras out of sight whenever possible;
- keep a low profile—avoid expensive or flashy clothing and do not advertise your itinerary in public;
- avoid wandering alone after dark;
- avoid dense crowds;
- consult your map and memorize your walking route through a town or city, then walk purposefully and confidently toward your destination;
- know where to find the embassy or consulate for your country and head there in case of serious emergency.

My adventure

During a lifetime of travel, I have been surprised and delighted by the kindness of strangers again and again. I have traveled alone in some notoriously dangerous places, confronted crocodiles, piranhas, storms, avalanches, floods, illness, and injury. In all those years I have had only one negative experience with a human being, and this one occurred in a civilized city, traveling with my husband, though temporarily alone.

I was wandering the back streets of Paris looking for photo opportunities while my husband, an artist, explored yet another museum. A man emerged from a café and fell into step beside me. He invited me for coffee. I refused. He didn't give up. He knew very little English; I knew very little French, but I pointed at my wedding ring, tried to explain that my husband was around the corner and that I was not interested. Then he began to make quick grabs and squeezes at various parts of my anatomy right out there on the street, desisting and adopting an innocent expression when other people were in sight. I kept cool and kept walking, but continued to push him away and angrily repeated, "No!" He began to sweat and grab more insistently. I headed back to the museum and he seemed to give up when I went inside. It was a big place and I couldn't locate my husband. I didn't know enough French to tell anybody what was wrong so I waited for about thirty minutes in the lobby, hoping my tormenter would give up. I peered out and couldn't see him so I walked out of the museum. As soon as I reached the bottom of the steps, he was back. This time, I steered him to the spot where we had parked our rented car, opened the door, pushed down the lock button, jumped inside, and slammed the door. The man was extremely agitated now, sweating and fogging the glass, scratching at the windows with his fingernails, looking crazed, but sane enough to back off and look innocent again whenever anybody came by. For what seemed like hours, I sat frozen in the sweltering, airless car, terrified that he would break a window and attack me. At last, he looked relieved, gave me a sickly smile, said "Ciao" and walked away.

8

Luggage and Packing

Every item you take with you should be selected for versatility and minimum weight. On conventional tours there is usually somebody around to handle your luggage. In the jungle or on the tundra, however, you'll be on your own. You must keep luggage light and compact enough to manage all of it by yourself. It is entirely possible to do this even for a journey of several weeks if you do it right.

Your luggage should consist of three basic components:
1. A travel wallet worn next to your skin for money and essential papers;
2. A daypack for carry-on items, emergency gear, film and valuable equipment like cameras;
3. A large duffel bag for everything else.

The travel wallet: Handbags and wallets carried in open pockets are easily snatched or slashed open, and you will want to have your hands free to do other things. A travel wallet can take the form of a soft belt with a flat envelope-like compartment worn around your waist, a pouch worn on a cord around your neck and tucked inside your clothing next to your chest, or a lightweight vest with lots of zippered compartments worn under other clothing. This keeps essential travel documents like passport, visas, credit cards, tickets, and money safe and secure, convenient, and out of sight, but easy to reach when you need them. The wallet should be comfortable so you can wear it all the time, it must seal shut with a zipper or Velcro, and it should be waterproof. There are a variety of fancy travel wallets available from travel goods stores, but if you have the time and/or talent, you can make your own out of any strong fabric and store your papers inside it in self-sealing plastic bags. Make sure it will stay on you and not come untied, unsnapped, or unzipped, but remember that you need to be able to get in and out of it yourself without half-undressing in public.

The daypack: This doubles as your carry-on bag while en route and your hands-free daily companion unless you will be backpacking with a larger standard backpack. Get a good quality, heavy-duty one, not the flimsy kind kids carry books to school in. Good ones are made of cordura, canvas, or rip-stop nylon with strong double-stitching on seams and shoulder straps. Shoulder straps should be padded for comfort, and if you will be carrying lots of heavy camera or other equipment, a padded waistband allows you to carry most of the weight on your hips, not on your shoulders. Into this pack goes:

a. Extra photocopies of important travel documents;
b. Camera(s) and film. (carry-on baggage x-ray machines in airports will not damage most kinds of film, but the heavy-duty machines that zap checked luggage might);
c. Other fragile, expensive gear you can't afford to have lost, stolen, damaged, or delayed in checked bags;
d. An emergency overnight kit with minimal toiletries; important prescription medicines; a few baby-wipes; a

quart of water preferably in a wide-mouthed, light-weight plastic thoroughly tested leakproof container; snacks such as high energy bars; a small flashlight, preferably a headlamp that allows you to keep your hands free (you might be getting out of the bus and setting up camp in the dark, and many developing countries are plagued by frequent power failures); and some extra clothing in case your other luggage is lost or delayed.

The duffel: A large, sturdy duffel bag rather than a hard, square suitcase is better for almost all forms of active travel. It is easier to stow in tight spaces in a van, a bus, or a bush plane, and is easier for human porters, yaks, or mules to carry. If you are traveling with an outfitter, most likely a duffel rather than a suitcase will be required. If you will be backpacking, stow your pack inside a duffel and lock it. Packs can't be locked and often have easily opened outside pockets. It is rare for luggage to be cut open or broken into, but a pocket that can be explored or emptied without a sign is often too tempting to resist. Besides, a sturdy duffel will save wear and tear on your pack.

Adventurers' luggage is likely to experience some very hard use. Your gear may be dropped, dragged, run over, trampled, or sunk. It should be of a heavy, rip-proof material like cordura or coated canvas, should be reinforced at vulnerable spots, have double-sewn seams with stitches that will not unravel, and heavy-duty zippers. Military ones from surplus stores serve very well, though they are not terribly convenient, since they open and close at only one end and must be unpacked completely to get at items on the bottom.

There are a few suitcase/backpack combinations on the market,—that is, suitcases that unfold to become backpacks (or backpacks that fold up to become suitcases)—but reviews have been mixed. Most backpackers who have tried them say they are not very comfortable over the long haul when fully loaded.

If your expedition involves a plane flight followed by some serious hiking, wear your boots on the plane. They are heavy to carry and awkward to pack, and you can't afford to lose them. Even if you will be able to buy new ones when you reach your destination, you probably won't have time to break them in, and blisters can spoil your entire vacation.

You might consider carrying on your sleeping bag as hand luggage as well. Good ones are very expensive to replace if available at all. Some trekkers in the Himalayas prefer to rent a bag when they arrive in a city like Kathmandu, but these may not be cleaned between one trek and the next.

PACKING TIPS

Allow plenty of time for packing. You may not be able to find necessary items you forgot at a wilderness trailhead or in a remote part of the world. Don't wait until the last minute to cram everything into your duffel and find it doesn't all fit, then jettison something important in the rush to make your flight. Packing early might bring to mind something else you need that is only available by mail order and may take time to arrive. If you are traveling with an outfitter, carefully check off everything on the list they will provide. They have been there before (or should have) and know what you will need. If the purpose of some piece of equipment is a mystery to you, ask what it is for. If it is on the list, it's probably necessary.

If you will be hiking, buy your boots months ahead of time to make sure they are well broken in. Take a couple of long, vigorous hikes up and down hills over rough terrain, preferably with some weight on your back. Walking around your house or on city sidewalks won't be enough. If you will be backpacking, this is especially important. Extra weight on your back puts extra stress on your feet.

If you will be using your own tent and will be setting it up by yourself, make sure to pitch it at least once at home before you leave. Make sure you have all the poles and stakes, especially if you have rented it. Even easy-to-follow directions won't help much in the dark, in wind, in rain, or, heaven forbid, all three!

If you are purchasing travel clothing or equipment by mail order, make sure you have time to receive it, try it, and exchange it if necessary.

GETTING IT ALL IN

Line your duffel with plastic trash bags if there is any chance of wet weather. Even luggage made of waterproof fabric can leak. This is especially important for your sleeping bag. Line its stuff sack with plastic before stuffing it.

To conserve space you can: Remove all unnecessary wrapping materials such as the cardboard boxes film comes in, plastic containers for batteries, and cellophane wrappers and cardboard sheets used to package clothing. If you will be carrying your own toilet paper (it isn't available in many places) remove the cardboard tube inside and flatten the roll. Put everything that needs protection into small plastic bags.

Use only small travel sizes of toiletries. Many grocery and drug stores carry tiny toothbrushes, toothpaste, deodorant, moisturizers, and shampoo. Bars of soap are messy and bulky. Instead use moist-towelettes or a small bottle of antiseptic, no-rinse soap you just rub in until it's dry. Cotton terrycloth washcloths and towels are also bulky, hard to dry, and will freeze stiff in cold weather. Instead, try Packtowls, which are very lightweight, super absorbent and fast-drying towel-substitutes sold by travel and outdoor equipment outfitters. Remember to seal all liquids in plastic bags, no matter how tight the lids seem to be. Changing air pressure on planes and rough handling anywhere can cause leaks. Avoid anything in aerosol cans, and keep important articles that could be damaged by moisture in plastic, too.

It should be apparent by now that you can never have too many plastic bags. Take a one-gallon size and pack into it an assortment of other sizes, from big lawn and leaf bags down to sandwich sizes.

Pack things inside other things. All sorts of small items will fit inside your shoes, cooking pots, or empty water bottles.

Pack your gear in several light, nylon stuff sacks of different colors so that you can identify the contents at a glance and to keep articles separate in your duffel. Keep underwear in one, toiletries in another, warm clothing in another, and books and field guides in yet another. If you have plenty, you can use an empty one for dirty laundry, or for storing separately your clean going-home clothes.

Assemble a little repair kit containing: a Swiss army knife or a Leatherman-type multi-purpose tool with scissors, saw, tweezers, screwdrivers, etc. Add a few yards of that all-purpose repair material, duct tape. You can wrap several yards of it around a pen or pencil, film canister, or water bottle. Don't waste extra space by tossing in a whole roll. Add a few safety pins of assorted sizes, a few rubber bands, a needle and thread. Two or three yards of coiled-up 20-gauge wire might come in handy in the backcountry as well. If you wear glasses, take extras, and take along a tiny eyeglass repair kit that comes complete with a magnifying glass, tiny screws, and a tiny screwdriver. Make sure that the screws are the right type and size for your glasses. There are an amazing variety of eyeglass screws and a ready-made kit might not work with yours specs at all. If you'll be physically active, Croakies or some other kind of cord fastened to the earpieces of your glasses will help keep them from being knocked off, dropped, or forgotten.

Even though you may be trying to get away from it all on your adventure vacation, you will need a watch to make plane/train or other schedules, to get yourself out of your bag or bed and to meals on time, and to judge distance on the trail. If you are traveling abroad, your internal biological clock will be confused and unreliable and you will need an alarm. If you're traveling with a group, other trip members will appreciate not having to wait for you. For real versatility, you can get a watch with a calculator for currency and/or metric conversions, and any number of other gadgets such as compasses, altimeters, and devices to measure your heart rate. (Carry a spare battery to keep all this stuff running, and know how to change it.) In fact, carry lots of batteries for any electronic devices you might be using including cameras, calculators, flashlights, tape recorders. Make sure they are the proper size and carry twice as many as you need. Fresh ones and odd sizes are hard to find in the Third World or in the wilderness. A handy hint: Remember that they don't work as well at low temperatures. If some electronic device fails in cold weather, try it again when it warms up before changing the battery. A second handy hint: Some countries are so nervous about terrorist activities that they will confiscate all batteries found in hand luggage for fear they may be used to make a bomb. Keep batteries in your checked luggage.

Airlines also prohibit bear-repellent spray, fully assembled firearms, and knives with blades longer than 3 inches (though sometimes even pocket knives may be confiscated).

If you will be backpacking and doing your own cooking, and if you will be traveling by air, be aware that cooking fuel of any kind is prohibited on planes. If your empty stove emits even the faintest whiff of fuel, you can't take it on board. Find out whether you will be able to get the kind of fuel your stove uses when you reach your destination, and if not, buy or borrow a different one. If you travel frequently, a mountaineering stove that uses several kinds of fuel is a good investment. Mountain Safety Research (MSR) makes the most popular one.

If you plan to take photos, you can never have too much film. Rolls of film are small and lightweight and you are bound to need more than you think. Even if you will be in towns where you can buy such things, the selection usually will be minimal, the freshness doubtful, and the price exorbitant.

A small notebook is invaluable for recording expenses, listing a few words in the local language, collecting names and addresses of people met along the way, or keeping track of photographs. Many travelers keep detailed daily journals to remind them of their adventures, to record sights, experiences, people, and their own reactions to everything. If you are a note taker or a letter or postcard writer, carry lots of extra pens. You're bound to lose, use up, or break a few.

SPECIALIZED EQUIPMENT

Your outfitter, if you are traveling with an organized group, may provide any specialized equipment you will need (e.g., kayak, canoe, dogsled), or, if not, will (or should) supply you with a detailed list of what you need to bring. Study it carefully and stick to it. Small items that may seem insignificant (or completely mysterious) to you could make all the difference between an exciting adventure and a painful ordeal.

If you plan to travel on your own, do your homework: consult people who have been there and done that before you. For example: For extreme cold, try lotions or creams, like Warmskin or Dermatone, that protect you from windburn, retard frostbite, and contain sunscreen. Don't forget lip balm with sunscreen in hot or cold climates. Will you need mosquito repellent or mosquito netting? In tropical, humid locales you might need to pack a desiccant, like silica gel, among personal belongings to absorb moisture and prevent or inhibit the growth of mold and mildew that can attack all sorts of surfaces, including your camera lenses. Will the footing be uneven or the stream crossings deep and dangerous? A lightweight, collapsible walking stick provides extra stability and confidence. On a water journey by raft, canoe, or kayak you may need one or more drybags, special rubberized bags that seal out water. What about ski wax, snorkel gear, bicycling or paddling gloves, climbing harness and hardware, or a helmet?

Once you have the necessities assembled and packed and determined that you will be able to handle it all, you can consider some of the wonderful gadgets available for adventurous travelers. Among the most popular are the solar shower, a black plastic bag with a hose and showerhead that can be filled with water, left out to warm in the sun during the day, and hung in a tree for a luxurious evening shower. Another is a contraption made of lightweight webbing and nylon into which you stuff your Therm-A-Rest or other self-inflating sleeping mat to form a comfy chair. Check out some of the catalogs in Appendix B for more ideas.

9

Clothing

Your priorities in clothing should be comfort and versatility. The well-dressed adventurer is rarely fashionable, unwrinkled, or squeaky clean.

If you will be traveling with an organized group, follow the guidelines the outfitters suggest. They have been there before (if they haven't, choose a different company) and know what works best for whatever you will be doing and the weather conditions in which you will be doing it.

Several lighter-weight layers are much better than fewer, heavier ones. You can add or remove layers as the temperature rises and falls and as you warm up from vigorous activity or cool down at rest. Even in cold climates you need to be able to remove layers before you become overheated and sweaty. Moisture of any kind, whether it comes from inside your clothing or out, whether from rain or from sweat, draws heat away from your body much faster than dry, open air at the same temperature does. Excessive sweating leads to dehydration which can seriously affect your energy and efficiency. Choose outer clothing roomy enough to wear over several other layers. In cold weather, too much tight, heavy clothing can restrict blood circulation and leave you colder than ever. In warm weather you'll need plenty of room for cool air to flow around you. In any temperature, too much bulky fabric can restrict your agility and freedom of movement.

Synthetic fabrics are almost always preferable to natural fibers. Cotton is not a good choice for most active travel and can be downright dangerous because it absorbs moisture and holds it next to your skin. Cotton also becomes heavy when it's wet and takes forever to dry. Synthetics like polypropylene or other "wicking" fibers draw moisture away from your skin and continue to insulate even when they are wet. They come in every conceivable weight from feather light (for use as underwear) to heavy pile or fleece. Wool is just as warm, but it is much heavier, especially when wet, and it dries very slowly. These synthetic fabrics are not windproof, so you will need to add a nylon shell in severe weather.

In warm weather as well as cold, blends of nylon and various kinds of polyester are great. They fit, breathe, and dry better than cotton. A new kind of specially treated cotton that can wick away moisture is under development, but hasn't yet been perfected.

You are not likely to be changing into clean clothes very often on an active wilderness adventure, so if visible dirt bothers you, wear colors and patterns that hide spots and blotches. Remember that dark colors absorb heat and lighter ones reflect it. Bright colors may attract insects. Military camouflage colors are a good compromise, but not recommended when traveling in places where there is a chance of political or civil unrest and/or a strong military presence.

Choose garments that can do double, or even triple duty. Underwear that is not too revealing can be used as a bathing suit. Long underwear makes comfy pajamas. You are not likely to have as much privacy on an expedition as you do at home, so even if you do not ordinarily sleep in any kind of clothing, think ahead. You could find yourself stumbling over sleeping bodies in darkness in the middle of the night trying to find something to wear for a quick trip to the toilet.

If your rain gear is made of a breathable fabric like Gore-Tex, you won't need to carry a windbreaker as well.

Buy pants with zippers around the thigh so you can change from long pants to shorts and back again.

Choose clothing with lots of pockets. Women may prefer to buy small men's sizes since they usually have more pockets.

No matter how warm the temperature, take a long-sleeved shirt to protect you from sunburn and insects.

If you plan to be doing a lot of walking, don't stint on socks. Dirty, sweaty ones can cause blisters. Most hard-core hikers wear two pairs: a lighter pair of liners underneath, and heavier socks over them. If your boots tend to rub, they should slide along the liners instead of your skin.

Colorful bandanas can be used as washcloths; as face protectors from wind, dust, or sun; as bandages or slings for first aid; as inexpensive gifts; or to blow your nose.

Take an extra pair of lightweight shoes in case of damage, blisters, or wet feet. Even if your boots are comfortable, a change of footwear can feel equivalent to a long rest.

Be sensitive to local custom when packing. Many cultures find bare legs and even arms offensive, especially for women. (More about this later.) In some Hindu countries where cows are sacred, the wearing of an animal product such as leather is prohibited in holy places. You can leave your shoes and belt outside, but will not want to abandon your wallet. If yours is made of leather, replace it with an inexpensive, lightweight one of Cordura or nylon while you are traveling.

For women, a lightweight, somewhat full long skirt with an elastic waist that can be slipped on over whatever else you're wearing at a moment's notice makes a handy cover-up.

SPECIAL CLOTHING FOR SPECIAL CLIMATES

Cold Weather

Layers of clothing are especially important in cold weather. The warmest material for the weight is down and there is nothing cozier at extreme temperatures. Unfortunately, it is useless if it becomes wet, so while it may be a good choice for the high dry Arctic or the Antarctic, it's not so great for travels in the rainforest of the Pacific Northwest where synthetics are more practical. A warm hat is probably the single most important item in your wardrobe in cold country since as much as half of your body heat is lost through your scalp because of the rich blood supply there. You will need two layers of warmth for your hands: lightweight liners for dexterity with heavier mittens to go over them. You might want waterproof mitts to go over the whole thing if you will be in wet country. In deep snow, you'll need gaiters to keep snow from going over the tops of your boots and melting into squelchy puddles inside. In blowing ice and snow a balaclava—which covers your head, face, and neck and has holes for your eyes and mouth—or a neoprene face mask helps protect against frostbite and windburn. Turtleneck shirts, clothes with hoods, and/or warm scarves or neck gaiters protect your neck where lots of blood flowing near the skin surface can make you cold. Boots for use in snow should have insulating liners that can be removed overnight to dry out, and should be roomy enough without cutting off your circulation.

Hot Weather

In hot weather a hat with a good brim all the way around will shade your eyes and help prevent sunburn. If you will be carrying a backpack, try on the hat and pack together to make sure one does not get in the way of the other. Broad-brimmed hats can sail away in a high wind unless secured with a cord under your chin. Try the foreign legion type with a bill in front and a flap (sometimes detachable) that protects the back of your neck. Keep skin covered with lightweight, light-colored clothing. Direct sun dries you out and overheats your surface, hastening dehydration. Consider the nomads of the world's great deserts who travel covered head to toe in loose, flowing robes.

My adventure

We had been touring the North Island of New Zealand for several days in a tiny car called a Riley through rolling green countryside dotted with sheep. The land was lovely but tame, and we craved vigorous exercise. When snow-capped Mt. Ruapehu appeared on the horizon, it drew us like a magnet. We left the main road, passed through an open, but strangely deserted, national park entrance, loaded our backpacks for an overnight climb and set off up the mountain. As we ascended, the temperature dropped dramatically and the rocks became dangerously icy. June is autumn in the southern hemisphere. We had not brought serious winter clothing or crampons with us and began to think better of our plan to spend the night on the mountain. We gave up, descended, and reached our car just at dark and camped in the deserted campground at the base of the mountain. Next day as we pulled out onto the highway, I glanced out the car window just in time to see the mountain belch out an enormous cloud of black smoke and ash and the summit dissolve as Mt. Ruapehu erupted. I have no idea whether we would have survived had we camped somewhere high on the mountainside.

10

Health

It should go without saying that you should start out healthy. Medical care is not easy to get in developing countries or in the wilderness. You should be clear about what physical challenges you will be facing and whether these might exacerbate any problems that are only minor in day-to-day life but could give big trouble if aggravated. If you have any doubts, get a check-up before you leave home. Have you seen your dentist recently? There may not be any on the mountain, up the river, or in the bush. Some remote localities are visited occasionally by traveling dentists. Since many of these places do not have electricity the dentist's drill is powered by a foot pump that he/she, an assistant, maybe even you, must operate.

A responsible outfitter, if you are traveling with one, should at least require you to fill out a questionnaire about your health and fitness, current medications, allergies, and any special medical conditions. Many will require that such a questionnaire be filled out and signed by your physician. Some provide a form describing the activities in which you will be engaging and the environment in which you will be traveling for your doctor to approve and sign. Keep in mind, of course, that a doctor serving an urban or suburban population may not be aware of the physical effects of, for example, extreme cold or high altitude, and has no way of predicting how such conditions will affect you if you haven't experienced them before.

GENERAL PREPARATIONS

The farther afield you intend to travel, the more physically challenging the activity you expect to engage in, and the fewer experienced companions or guides are with you, the more homework you'll need to do beforehand, the more extensive your first-aid kit, and the more detailed your medical handbook needs to be. Unfamiliar environments can bring unexpected health problems. Travel at high elevation, for example, or gaining elevation too quickly, can be severely debilitating. If you have not traveled at high altitude before and do not know how susceptible you are to its effects, you need to be able to prevent, recognize, and treat altitude sickness, especially those (fortunately rare) forms that can be fatal.

Check your medical insurance or HMO policy to find out whether you are covered in foreign countries. (If you are on Medicare, you are not covered.) Find out whether you are covered for emergency evacuation by helicopter, for example, whether at home or abroad, and if you are not, ask your travel agent about special short-term travelers insurance.

Be realistic about your physical conditioning. If a guided adventure is listed as "moderately strenuous," you should understand exactly what that means. If the literature isn't clear, ask specific questions: How many miles/hours per day, over what kind of terrain, at what elevation, in what kind of weather? An "easy" climb/ride/paddle means different things to people who do it often and those who are sedentary most of the time. If you are not quite as physically fit as you should be, don't wait until a month before your departure to begin your conditioning program. You'll have a much better time if you're not exhausted and will be a better traveling companion if others do not have to wait for you.

IMMUNIZATIONS

Public agencies like local or state health departments, embassies, and HMOs that have travel immunization services know what shots are required or recommended for just about any destination in the world. Most of their information comes from the Centers for Disease Control (CDC) and the World Health Organization (WHO). You can get this information directly from these organizations yourself. (See Appendix B.)

Another excellent source of information is the IAMAT (International Association for Medical Assistance to Travelers). Membership is free of charge (though donations are gratefully accepted). They issue a directory of English-speaking physicians who have agreed to a set fee schedule for members in 125 countries. They also publish a chart advising on immunizations for countries all over the world, as well as information about high-risk areas for specific diseases such as malaria and schistosomiasis. They'll even tell you what schistosomiasis is. (See Appendix B.)

Along with information about what special health hazards are to be found in various parts of the world, these organizations publish all kinds of gory details about how diseases are transmitted (if you really want to know), how to avoid them, and how to recognize symptoms. They publish maps showing the geographic range of various diseases and updates on current outbreaks, along with suggestions about what kinds of medicines and health care supplies to carry with you.

Be sure to allow plenty of time to get everything you need, roughly six to eight weeks before departure. Some immunizations require several doses administered months apart, and some cannot be given in combination with others. Anti-malarial agents must be started before you leave and continued for some time after you return.

For domestic or international travel, make sure your tetanus immunization is up to date.

MALARIA

Malaria gets a special section of its own because so many places offering exciting adventures are in the tropics where it constitutes a serious health hazard. Anopheles mosquitoes, malaria's carriers and transmitters, have been called the heroes of tropical rain forest conservation since the presence of the disease has discouraged settlement in and development of these areas. Malaria has been eradicated in some parts of the world in recent years by the use of DDT, but with serious consequences to the environment. Check with your doctor, health agency, the CDC, or the WHO to find out whether you will need anti-malarial drugs where you are going, and which ones are effective for the strains of the disease there. New drugs are constantly being developed and prescribed as the parasite develops resistance to the old ones. Keep in mind that you must begin your malaria protection before you leave, never miss a dose, and continue for the prescribed period after you return. Even so, the drugs are not 100 percent effective, so try to avoid being bitten in the first place. Keep skin covered and use DEET (N, N-diethyl-meta-toluamide), the active ingredient in many bug repellents. It is the only really effective repellent. DEET is fairly safe to use in concentrations of less than 30 percent, and it's a whole lot safer than malaria. Other DEET-less preparations are available, but are only marginally effective.

The symptoms of malaria are chills, fever, and headaches, all severe. It can feel like the flu in the beginning, and may not show up for several months after you have been exposed, so check it out if you feel like you're coming down with something after you get home. There is effective treatment for malaria if it is detected early, but if left untreated, it can have serious consequences.

THE FIRST-AID KIT

This is essential whether traveling with an outfitter or alone. If you're on your own, your kit must be much more extensive, of course, and must go a bit beyond first aid. First aid is defined as caring for illness or injury until professional help arrives. In a remote place where no professional help can be expected, or at least not for a long time, you'll need more sophisticated supplies and equipment, and more important, more knowledge. Some of what you need, of course, will depend on where you're going. The following are suggestions only and not to be considered a definitive list:

- Adhesive bandages
- Sunscreen
- Mosquito repellent
- Iodine or other water disinfectant
- Alcohol wipes
- Gauze
- Tape
- Splint
- Elastic bandages
- Thermometer
- Oral rehydration solution
- Rubber gloves
- Syringes (in case you need a shot in some remote spot where needles may be contaminated)

Over-the-Counter Drugs:

- Antihistamines for allergies
- Dramamine for motion sickness or nausea
- Topical antibiotics (Neosporin, Polysporin)
- Hydrocortisone
- Antifungus preparations, especially where it's hot and humid
- Cough medicine
- Diarrhea medicine
- Mild laxatives
- Anti-inflammatories like ibuprofin

Prescription Drugs:

- Antibiotics such as Cipro, Keflex

- Anti-protozoan (Giardia, amoebas) preparations such as Flagyl
- Personal prescriptions (If any of these are narcotics or drugs requiring injection, make sure to carry a spare copy of the prescription or a letter from your physician authorizing their use.)
- Bee sting or other antihistamine kit, if you are allergic
- A detailed wilderness or travel medicine book (This is especially important if you're on your own. There are several good ones listed in Appendix B.)

EN ROUTE

Jet lag plagues luxury, business, and adventure travelers alike. There's not too much you can do about it except allow yourself time to adjust. The more time zones you cross, the longer adjustment takes. This is especially important for adventure travelers to be aware of since it can decrease your resistance to disease and can affect your physical performance. If your trip involves strenuous activity, you especially want to be well and rested. Experts say your body cannot adjust much faster than an hour in a day, so the more time you have between landing and beginning strenuous activity the better. You can help the process along by sleeping (with the use of a sleep mask and earplugs if necessary) during part of your normal sleep cycle while en route.

Motion sickness is very unlikely during jet travel, but much more common on small planes, boats, or motorized ground transport. If you are subject to it, or do not know whether you are, there are over-the-counter remedies like

Dramamine that are quite effective, though they make most people drowsy. Take these before you embark; if you wait until you're already nauseated, you might not be able to keep them down. There are skin patches available, too. You are less likely to suffer nausea on a full stomach than an empty one, strange though it may seem, and drinking plenty of water is helpful, too. Avoid reading while in motion, avoid the rear section of vehicles, and, if possible, get plenty of fresh air.

WHEN YOU GET THERE

A great many diseases in developing countries can be traced to inadequate sanitation. The local folks don't prefer dirt, but may lack the simplest of facilities. Often villagers (usually women) must walk many miles to fetch water, then carry it home again. There is never enough to drink, cook with, and bathe in. There are no sewers or waste treatment plants. Soil and ground water become contaminated. There are frequently no public health agencies, at least effective ones, and there is no money to correct problems even when they are recognized.

Your first line of defense as a traveler is cleanliness. Carry plenty of disposable moist towelettes or more environmentally friendly anti-bacterial waterless soap.

By far the most common problem is diarrhea. The WHO estimates that 20 to 50 percent of all travelers will contract it. On the other hand, illness is not inevitable. The majority of travelers do not get sick. Adventure travelers who are less likely to be staying in western-style accommodations are more at risk, of course. They are usually more likely to agree that one of the great pleasures of traveling is being invited into someone's home to share a meal prepared under questionable conditions and/or being prodded or hugged by grubby little hands belonging to grubby, usually runny-nosed little kids.

The usual dose of tourist trots or Delhi belly is no more than a passing nuisance anyway, though amoebic dysentery and some other forms of food poisoning can be very serious indeed. Should you be stricken, even with a mild case, drink lots and lots of clean water. The greatest threat to your health, whether from the garden-variety tourist crud or from a serious gastrointestinal infection, is dehydration. The most urgent and important treatment for fluid loss due to diarrhea or vomiting is rehydration, adding oral rehydration salts if the symptoms are prolonged and severe. If there is blood or mucus in the stool and the problem persists more than a couple of days, you will need to take antibiotics or antiprotozoan agents. Do not take drugs that shut down all intestinal activity (like Lomotil) unless you become so debilitated from dehydration that you cannot keep moving or get to medical help.

AIDS is, of course, a worldwide epidemic, and is rampant in developing countries. Take the usual precautions, but much more so when away from home. Avoid injections or transfusions, unless death will be immediate and certain otherwise, and do not indulge in unprotected sex.

WATER

Treat or avoid all water unless it comes in a sealed bottle or container. That includes wild-flowing streams and lakes, tap water, ice cubes, and any drinks served by the glass. It's nice to know that coffee, tea, soft drinks, and beer are (usually) safe beverages. (Some water can get you into trouble just by standing in it. The parasite called schistosomiasis mentioned earlier lives in fresh water, gets into your body through your skin, and wreaks all kinds of havoc on various internal organs.)

If you are traveling with an outfitter, make sure they are adequately treating the water you are using. To be safe, just treat your own. Boiling water rapidly for about ten minutes will kill just about anything nasty. Most organisms are killed long before that time.

Iodine is easy to carry and also very effective, though a few people have allergic reactions to it. It comes in many forms. Iodine tablets are fine as long as they are fresh, but once the container is opened, they lose their potency rapidly. Do not keep a bottle from one year to the next. Tincture of iodine is safer. Use two to five drops per quart and let stand twenty minutes, unless the water is extremely cold or extremely ugly. Then use more and let it stand longer. Chlorine is somewhat effective, but greater quantities and more time are needed. There are many good water filters available, but only a few give effective protection from viruses. If you plan to rely on one, make sure it is guaranteed against viruses. (If it is, it's probably because it has iodine as a component.) Furthermore, filters can get clogged and lose their effectiveness over time. Make sure you know how to clean it and take extra parts. Boiling and iodine are best.

FOOD

Make sure all meat and vegetables are well cooked. Raw fruits and vegetables that can be peeled are safe, as are foods that have been soaked in iodine-treated water. The usual rule is: "Boil it, cook it, peel it, or forget it." You'll survive without any serious vitamin deficiencies for a few weeks without eating salads. On the other hand, one of the pleasures of travel is tasting new foods. You will have to decide whether you are willing to make compromises between getting sick, enjoying a new experience, and committing a social blunder by refusing to accept some proffered delicacy in order to stay healthy.

One last word of caution: While you are avoiding biting into anything unwholesome, take care to avoid being bitten by anything yourself: bugs, mammals, or people. Rabies is a very real danger in many developing countries.

My adventure

In Bombay, weak from dehydration as a result of amoebic dysentery, I passed out on a street corner. I was gently helped up, fanned, and fussed over by a kind group of Indian pedestrians. One rushed away and returned with a glass of water (probably teeming with more amoebas) presented on a little paper doily on a silver tray.

AFTER THE TRIP

If you think you might have been exposed to any exotic diseases or come down with any suspicious symptoms after your trip, even months later, be sure to let your physician know where you have been. Many potentially serious problems can be diagnosed by a simple blood test and easily treated.

11

Travel Insurance

If you plan to travel in an organized group with a commercial (or nonprofit) outfitter, you will probably be required to make a substantial deposit when you sign up and will have to hand over the balance at the very least several days before you depart. Even if you will be traveling on your own, international airfare can be expensive, and the earlier you buy your ticket, the cheaper the fare. If you cannot afford to lose what you have already invested if you should be forced to cancel your trip, by all means, purchase trip cancellation insurance. If your adventure will take you to some remote region far from medical facilities, whether alone or with a group, you should also investigate a package that includes medical evacuation insurance as well. In fact, some adventure travel companies make it a requirement.

Even if you are always healthy and believe that nothing could possibly cause you to cancel or interrupt your adventure, insurance covers circumstances over which you may have no control. These might include: losing or being laid off from your job; being called for jury duty; being called up for military service; being robbed, assaulted, or hospitalized within ten days of your trip; having an accident on the way to the airport; or learning from the State Department that your destination has been declared unsafe for travel. Some policies will even reimburse you if the outfitter or the airline you signed up with goes bankrupt.

Be sure to read the fine print. Medical and emergency evacuation insurance usually excludes activities like technical mountain climbing, skydiving, hang-gliding, scuba diving, piloting a small plane, or participating in a race. Read all about those pre-existing conditions; you will not be covered if you are pregnant, crazy, or drunk. It is usually required that you sign up for travel insurance at the time, or a few days after, you make your trip reservations.

You can buy travel insurance in all sorts of combinations: cancellation insurance alone, medical evacuation alone, or in a complete package that includes lost luggage and other contingencies. You may pay a flat premium based on the number of days you will be traveling and the amount of coverage you want, or you may be charged on a basis of anywhere from $5 to $10 dollars per each $100 you spend on the trip. On average, travel insurance for a 30-day expedition overseas will cost about $200 to $300.

Some of the large adventure travel companies include an insurance package in the cost of the trip (though you have the right to refuse it). Many work with a travel insurance company and can help you sign up. Note that some companies make medical evacuation insurance mandatory for treks in remote places like the Himalayas or Kilimanjaro. Check the Internet or see your travel agent for more information.

12

Red Tape: Passports, Visas, and Permits

A passport is required for international travel, and visas are required for visits of more than a day or so in many countries. You must apply for your first passport in person, but it will be valid for ten years, and after the first one, you can apply by mail.

Allow plenty of time—several months—to get your passport. Even if you are casually considering international travel at some indefinite date in the future, do it now. The wheels of government turn slowly.

If you will be going someplace where a visa is needed, you will have to send your passport to the consulate or embassy or to a visa agency that will do it for you. Then you must allow the wheels of *that* country's government to do their slow turning to issue, attach, or stamp the visa to your passport and return it to you.

Important: If you have already had your passport for a number of years, make sure it won't expire while you are still traveling or you'll have a hard time getting back into the United States. Furthermore, some governments require that your passport be valid for six months after the date you plan to leave the country. Do your arithmetic carefully. You could be refused entry into the country after spending lots of money on airfare to get there. Airlines do ask to see your passport when you check in, but their only responsibility is to make sure that your passport is valid at the time you board the plane.

HOW TO APPLY FOR YOUR FIRST PASSPORT

First, contact the State Department by telephone or check the Internet for addresses of the regular passport agencies. (There are only thirteen of these.) You can also go to one of the many federal or state courthouses or post offices that handle passports. You will need to take with you:

1. Proof of Citizenship in the form of a certified copy of your birth certificate (not just a photocopy) or, if you were not born in the United States, a Certificate of Naturalization.
2. Two photographs taken within the past six months, 2 x 2 inches in size. The kind you get from a vending machine are not acceptable. Order two or three sets of photos while you're at it. You may need more for visas or as extras if you lose your passport.
3. Proof of Identity: A driver's license will do.
4. A check for $65.
5. Your Social Security number.

Hand over all these documents, fill out the application form, then wait for your passport to come by mail.

GETTING A NEW PASSPORT

If you already have a passport or have had one issued within the past twelve years, you can get a new one by mail. Pick up an application at a passport agency, courthouse, post office, or travel agency. Fill it out, enclose your old passport, two photos, and a check for $55, and mail it in. They will return your old cancelled passport along with the new one.

Contact the State Department for procedures for getting a passport in a hurry, traveling with children, or changing your name.

WILDERNESS PERMITS

In the United States, many national parks, national forests and state parks require visitors to obtain a wilderness permit for an overnight stay in a wilderness area. Sometimes these are free; sometimes there is a nominal charge. Permits help the agency responsible for the land keep track of how much use a particular area gets in order to most efficiently allot (and request) funds and assign personnel for maintenance. In popular areas whose wild qualities are threatened by overuse, an agency might set quotas on the number of permits issued.

Each agency seems to have a different procedure and different regulations for issuing permits, so you will need to find out who is in charge and what they require. Do this well in advance of your proposed adventure. In some cases you can just drop in to the ranger station nearest the trailhead, fill out a form, and hit the trail. In other cases, a certain percentage, usually 50 percent, of permits to enter the wilderness on a given day are available by mail perhaps sixty or ninety days prior to departure, and the other 50 percent are granted on a first come, first served basis. Some agencies governing very fragile and/or overused places have wait lists of one to ten years. Others issue permits only by lottery.

When you apply for a permit, you must state the day and place you plan to enter and leave the wilderness, and sometimes furnish an estimated itinerary. Your signature on this permit does not mean that you have hired local rangers as babysitters. Nobody will come looking for you if you do not return on time unless you have left word with someone at home to do so. If you do not show up as expected, friends or relatives can contact the ranger station to begin a search based on the information on your permit.

13

For Women Only

Until very recent times, the typical adventure traveler has been male. The few women who participated in exploration of distant lands or performed feats of physical strength and endurance on mountain peaks, in steaming jungles, or across icy wastes usually did so as wives, seldom as leaders or solo travelers. There have been notable exceptions, of course, but they are notable because they are exceptions. Many of those intrepid women had to disguise themselves as men to get where they wanted to go and do what they wanted to do.

There is no reason whatsoever that women at this time in human history should have greater difficulty or find less satisfaction in adventure than men. (Was it Dorothy Parker who pointed out that Ginger Rogers could do everything Fred Astaire could, but that she could do it backwards and in high heels?) In the past, women constantly burdened with pregnancy or children certainly had other priorities, but even in bygone days they did manage to cross mountains and deserts, endure deprivations and hardships, and bear and raise children at the same time. In fact, women in nomadic cultures still do it. Contemporary women have choices, and even those who choose to raise families can expect to live long past the time when that task is done and can set out to explore the world beyond the hearth.

Still the tradition, the habit, of caution persists among women along with the belief that they are not suited to certain kinds of strenuous outdoor activities. They need to remember that most of these activities do not depend upon brute strength alone, but require finesse, flexibility, courage, persistence, and patience, characteristics women possess in abundance. Women are rapidly establishing themselves among males as superb athletes in sport after sport. They excel in climbing, where agility and finesse are as valuable as physical strength, and in managing animals, from horses to huskies, where patience and love get better results than force. There is some evidence that women are more resistant to altitude sickness than men. Women's slightly higher percentage of body fat may give them a narrow advantage over men in their ability to survive extreme cold and hunger, and they are capable of bearing more pain (not that this is the goal of anybody's vacation!).

If you are unsure of your own physical or emotional fitness, are still mired in lifelong habits of dependency on men, or simply enjoy the company of other women, try a trip designed for women only. These may or may not be any less physically demanding than coed outings, but, as a rule, other women are more likely to be supportive of one another, to be willing to help each other learn and grow and meet challenges without the added pressure of competition. Many expedition outfitters offer adventures for women only, and many others are owned and operated by and for women.

Aside from physiological considerations, women have to deal with a different set of social and cultural challenges, especially, but not exclusively, in foreign parts. As always, do your research before you leave home. Cultural sensitivity on somebody else's turf is crucial for anybody of either sex who wants to get the most out of a travel experience, but becoming informed may be necessary to a woman's safety. While most western women may be liberated, women elsewhere are not. You may be confident and capable of even solo travel to other parts of the world, but the women who live there haven't come so far, and you can't expect to behave and be treated as you are at home. Find out what the status of women is in the place you plan to visit, and whether the attitudes found in big cities differ from those in rural villages. In some societies, women are believed to be something less than human and may even be thought dangerous to the spiritual well-being of men who might be tempted into sin by their charms. (In a Coptic monastery on a little island in Lake Tana in Ethiopia, for example, fresh eggs are delivered daily by reed boats to the monks who live there since the company of female animals, even *chickens,* is forbidden.)

In some parts of the world, the only women who appear in public unescorted are prostitutes. If your travels take you to some really remote places where this is the case, do not be surprised if you are treated accordingly. Even in countries "developed" enough to have television, the locals' only exposure to western manners and mores may come from the television. Americans in particular are perceived to be murderous sex maniacs. While your dress and behavior may be perfectly proper, locals might already have made (mistaken) assumptions about you, and might be surprised when you angrily reject sexual advances. Behavior on your part meant to be simply open and friendly may be interpreted as a come-on. Watch what local women do. You'll probably find it easier to approach and make friends with them than with men (as long as your behavior doesn't threaten or embarrass them). Women the world over share family concerns and are curious about one another's daily lives. Just remember that women in many societies, having been exposed to no other system of belief accept, for the most part, their own lowly status. Do not expect sympathy from local women if you flaunt what they perceive to be indecent standards of dress or behavior.

Consider the effect your behavior might have on other women who come after you. Your too-casual dress or attitude could reinforce the message that western women are easy prey and bring trouble to the next woman who arrives, even if she is the soul of circumspection.

If you do not think you will be able to tolerate sexist attitudes and behavior, stay away. Consider, however, that if the purpose of your journey is education and personal growth, exposure to the condition of women in other parts of the world may arouse your indignation to the point where you will become motivated to do something about it. Just remember that you alone are not going to bring about fundamental changes in another society during the course of your vacation.

A more practical approach might be to follow the example of many trekkers in Nepal. Trekkers often form warm friendships with their Nepali guides whose warmth and hospitality are legendary. In that country, if a village can raise the money to build a schoolhouse, the government will provide a teacher. Travelers often raise money (usually paltry sums by western standards) to help build schools in their Nepali friends' villages with the stipulation that girls, who are usually excluded, be allowed to attend.

SAFETY MEASURES

- Dress conservatively. In many parts of the world women do not expose much skin. Bare arms as well as legs are offensive. Carry something with long sleeves along with a long skirt you can slip on over other clothing when necessary. A bandana tucked into your pocket might come in handy in getting you into places where women keep their heads covered.

- Adopt a confident and purposeful, though not aggressive, attitude and posture. Women (and men) who walk briskly and purposefully, heads up, are much less likely to be accosted than those who give off "victim" vibes by their tentative, uncertain manner. When navigating a new city, for example, study your map and determine your route first, then set out confidently toward your goal.

- Do not wear expensive jewelry, display large amounts of cash in public, or flaunt expensive cameras or electronic equipment any more than is absolutely necessary. Statistically, outside the west, women are more likely to be victims of robbery than of rape. In fact, in some Middle Eastern countries, it is illegal for a man to touch a woman in public.

- Remember what your mother told you about getting into vehicles or going to secluded places with strange men. The fact that you are on vacation and feeling free and footloose does not mean it is safe to abandon the usual precautions you would take in your own environment. Also remember that no matter how liberated a woman you may be, your feminism will not protect you from aggression in an unliberated country (or even in a liberated one).

- Maintain a low profile and do not travel alone if you can help it. Women who do travel alone often find they are taken under the wings of other travelers and natives alike because they are believed to need protection. If you don't find this unbearably objectionable and insulting, take advantage of it. You might find that you will have access to places and practices normally denied to foreign women and may make wonderful new friends to boot.

HEALTH AND HYGIENE HINTS

- Your normal menstrual cycle will probably go haywire

because of time changes, unaccustomed exercise, and general stress. It's no big thing, but be prepared. Carry plenty of tampons or whatever product you use. They are not available in many parts of the world. Carry lots of plastic bags, too, since it might be difficult or at least awkward to dispose of them. Remember to take yeast medicine, especially in places where you may be exposed to infection. Prolonged use of some antibiotics kill the good bugs as well as the bad ones and may leave you vulnerable to yeast.

- If you take birth control pills, remember that they carry a minor risk of blood clots in extremities that can travel to your lungs. Long periods of inactivity, such as sitting for many hours on a long flight, can present problems if you are susceptible.

- It should go without saying that pregnancy is an additional, if minor, risk. If you have any reason to expect complications, postpone your travel. Also be aware that medical travel insurance will not cover you if you are pregnant.

- Some serious athletes such as climbers embarking on an extended ascent or explorers on a prolonged polar expedition take birth control pills continuously for one or two cycles to prevent the inconvenience of menstruation. Check with your doctor first.

My adventure

I was standing in the empty Algiers airport at 4:00 AM in order to catch a 7:00 AM flight to Addis Ababa via Rome. I was there three hours early because the guide of the Sahara camel safari I had been with for the past two weeks warned that whether one has a confirmed ticket or not, it's first come, first served when it comes to getting boarding passes. I made sure I would be first in line.

Other passengers began to trickle in. I had already learned during years of travel in developing countries that the custom of politely forming a neat line and taking one's turn is a purely western invention. I had become fairly adept at surviving the battle of the elbows and line-cutting over the years, but this time it was different. I was the only woman in a rapidly filling room of male Arabs. Women are nonpersons in this part of the world, no more than property, and invisible.

By 6:00 I found myself at the wrong end of a very long line of men who, somehow, without actually jostling or shoving me, had insinuated themselves in front of me. I simply cannot explain it. I must have been half-asleep while it was happening. I finally woke up to the fact that I was not going to get onto this overbooked flight.

What to do? Seek out official help? I couldn't see anybody who looked official, and officials would probably be Arab men, too. Should I kick and punch my way to the front of the line? Burst into tears? Neither would be effective and might be outright dangerous. I began to panic.

All at once, at the last minute, a miracle! The crowd in front of me parted like the Red Sea. Not one man made eye contact, but it was obvious that I was to move forward. Amazed, I grabbed my bags and scuttled toward the counter to a position second in line, just behind the only sandy-colored, non-turbaned head in the place. I hadn't noticed him before in the crush. I looked at him. "Wha . . . ?" "Later," he hissed out of the corner of his mouth. I shut up, picked up my boarding pass, and followed him onto the plane.

Safely buckled in, I asked him what had happened. He said he had turned to the man next to him and said quietly, "You're pushing my woman." That's all it took. In a culture where politely asking somebody how the wife and kiddies are doing is enough to get your throat cut, touching somebody else's female property is a heinous crime.

That time, I swallowed my feminist indignation, thanked the gods that chivalry was not dead, and bought my hero, an Englishman employed by an oil company in Africa, the finest dinner available in Rome.

Appendix A: An Adventurous Traveler's Checklist

The essentials (whatever the mode of transportation or accommodation—hotel, cabin, or tent):

Flashlight

Extra batteries

Plastic bags of all sizes

Toilet paper

Waterless soap/baby wipes

Swiss army knife or equivalent with tweezers, scissors, nail file, corkscrew

Water containers to hold minimum of one quart

Iodine for water purification

Reliable travel alarm clock

Ear plugs

Sleep mask

Extra passport photos

Extra copies of first page of passport

Sunglasses, sunscreen, lip balm

Energy bars

Toiletries in small sample sizes: toothbrush, toothpaste, deodorant, shaving materials, waterless soap, moisturizer, small brush or comb, shampoo

Lightweight small towel such as a Packtowl

Notions like: Safety pins, rubber bands, needle and thread, duct tape, eyeglass kit, a bit of 20 gauge wire and/or twenty feet or so of light nylon cord for hanging clothes or emergency repairs

First aid kit, especially foot care (see health chapter)

Personal prescriptions

Clothing for a walking trip of two to three weeks:

2–3 long- and short-sleeved shirts

2–3 pairs long and short pants

Long overskirt for women

Underwear

Nightwear (long underwear)

Bathing suit if appropriate

3–4 pairs socks

2 pairs shoes, one for daily walking, one for camp

Sun hat

Warm hat

Bandanas

Rain gear; jacket and pants are better than a poncho

Medium weight sweater or jacket

Warm jacket

Special needs for special places:

Buggy places:
Insect repellent
Mosquito netting
Headnet

Cold or snowy places:
Gaiters
Balaclava
Down parka
Long underwear
Warm gloves, mittens

For complete self-sufficiency, tent camping or backpacking:

Sleeping bag
Insulating pad
Tent with rainfly
Stove and fuel

Cooking pot
Cup, spoon
Matches, lighter
Map, compass

Optional items:

Walking stick(s)
Camera and film
Tape recorder
Binoculars

Field guides
Foreign language dictionary
Small notebook and several pens

Appendix B: Resources

BOOKS

Adventurous Traveler
Bookstore
P.O. Box 64769
Burlington, VT 05406
800-282-3963
www.adventuroustraveler.com

FalconGuides and Insiders
Guides
Falcon Publishing
P.O. Box 1718
Helena, MT 59624
800-725-8303
www.falcon.com

Medicine for the Outdoors
Paul S. Auerbach, M.D.
Little, Brown and Company;
1991

Medicine for Mountaineering
James A. Wilkerson, M.D.
The Mountaineers; Seattle,
1992

Wilderness First Aid
Gilbert Preston, M.D.
Falcon; Helena, MT, 1997

The World's Most Dangerous
Places
Robert Young Pelton et al.
Fielding Worldwide, Inc.;
Redondo Beach, CA, 1998

Volunteer Vacations
Bill McMillon
Chicago Review Press;
Chicago 1993

A Journey of One's Own
Thalia Zepatos
The Eights Mountain Press;
1996

HEALTH AND SAFETY
RESOURCES

Centers for Disease Control
(CDC)
1600 Clifton Rd., NE #4065
Atlanta, GA 30329
404-639-1603
www.cdc.gov/travel

World Health Organization
(WHO)
CH-1211
Geneva 27
Switzerland
www.who.int

International Association for
Medical Assistance to
Travelers (IAMAT)
417 Center St.
Lewiston, NY 14092
716-754-4883
www.sentex.net/~iamat

Overseas Citizens Services
Room 4811
Department of State
Washington, DC 20520
www.travel.state.gov

OUTFITTERS

Specialty Travel Index (guide
to outfitters)
305 San Anselmo Ave.
San Anselmo, CA 94960
415-459-4900
www.spectrav.com

Reality Tours
Global Exchange
2017 Mission St. #303
San Francisco, CA 94110
800-255-7498
www.globalexchange.org

Earthwatch Institute
680 Mt. Auburn St.
P.O. Box 9104
Watertown, MA 02471
617-926-8200
www.earthwatch.org

Elderhostel
75 Federal St.
Boston, MA 02110
877-426-8056
www.elderhostel.org

Hostelling International-
American Youth Hostels
733 15th St. NW
Washington, DC 20005
202-783-6161
800-444-6111
www.hiayh.org

Backroads Bicycle Touring
801 Cedar St.
Berkeley, CA 94710
800-462-2848
www.backroads.com

Zegraham Expeditions
(Astronaut training)
192 Nickerson St. #200
Seattle, WA 98109
800-628-8747
www.zeco.com

W.I.L.D. (Domestic & international natural science trips)
P.O. Box 8397
Van Nuys, CA 91409
818-781-4421
www.inetworld.net/wild

Goodwaters Adventures
(Himalayan Treks)
831 W. California Ave. #P
Sunnyvale, CA 94086
408-774-1257
Nepaltreks@aol.com

Wintermoon/Summersun
Adventures (dogsledding,
hiking, canoeing for women)
3388 Petrell
Brimson, MN 55602
218-848-2442

Mountain Travel/Sobek
6420 Fairmount Ave.
El Cerrito, CA 94530
888-MTSOBEK
www.mtsobek.com

Blue Waters Kayaking
P.O. Box 983
Inverness, CA 94937
888-865-9288
www.bwkayak.com

Wilderness Travel
1102 Ninth St.
Berkeley, CA 94710
800-368-2794
www.wildernesstravel.com

Remote River Expeditions
Box 59622
Nairobi, Kenya
800-558-1083

National Outdoor Leadership
School (NOLS)
288 Main St.
Lander, WY 82520
307-332-5300
www.nols.edu

Sierra Club
85 Second St., Second Floor
San Francisco, CA 94105
415-977-5500
www.sierraclub.org

Appalachian Mountain Club
5 Joy St.
Boston, MA 02108
617-523-0655
www.outdoors.org

ENVIRONMENTAL WATCHDOG ORGANIZATIONS

The International
Ecotourism Society
P.O. Box 755
North Bennington, VT
05257
802-447-2121
www.ecotourism.org

RARE Center for Tropical
Conservation
1616 Walnut St. #1010
Philadelphia, PA 19103
215-735-3510
e-mail: rare@rarecenter.org

RESOURCES FOR DISABLED TRAVELERS

The Guided Tour, Inc.
7900 Old York Rd. #114B
Elkins Park, PA 19027
800-783-5841
www.guidedtour.com

Mobility International USA
(MIUSA)
P.O. Box 10767
Eugene, OR 97440
541-343-1284
www.miusa.org

Access First News
Newsletter of: Access First
Travel
239 Commercial St.
Malden, MA 02148
800-557-2047

About the Author

Suzanne Swedo has conducted wilderness survival, outdoor skills, and natural science outings for over twenty years as founder and director of W.I.L.D., an international and domestic adventure travel company. She has also led trips for nonprofit educational organizations, including Wilderness Institute, Pacific Wilderness Institute, Outdoor Adventures, Sierra Club, and University of California Extension. She teaches backcountry natural history seminars for the Yosemite Association in Yosemite National Park, and hosted to the ten-week television series *Alive and Well.* Her writings on survival have appeared in such publications as the *Los Angeles Examiner* and *California* magazine. Suzanne has also written *Hiking Yosemite, Best Easy Day Hikes Yosemite,* and *Wilderness Survival;* all published by Falcon Publishing.